Francis Frith's
HAMPSHIRE

◆

PHOTOGRAPHIC MEMORIES

Francis Frith's
HAMPSHIRE

◆

Nick Channer

First published in the United Kingdom in 1999
by Frith Book Company Ltd
ISBN 1-85937-064-0

Reprinted in Hardback 2001

Paperback edition 2001
ISBN 1-85937-279-1

Reprinted in Paperback 2002, 2004

British Library Cataloguing in Publication Data

Hampshire
Nick Channer
ISBN 1-85937-279-1

Frith Book Company Ltd
Frith's Barn, Teffont,
Salisbury, Wiltshire SP3 5QP
Tel: +44 (0) 1722 716 376
Email: info@francisfrith.co.uk
www.francisfrith.co.uk

Printed and bound in Great Britain

Front Cover: **ROMSEY**, *Old Corn Exchange 1932* 85040

*The colour-tinting is for illustrative purposes only, and is not intended
to be historically accurate*

CONTENTS

FRANCIS FRITH: *Victorian Pioneer*

FRANCIS FRITH, Victorian founder of the world-famous photographic archive, was a complex and multitudinous man. A devout Quaker and a highly successful Victorian businessman, he was both philosophical by nature and pioneering in outlook.

By 1855 Francis Frith had already established a wholesale grocery business in Liverpool, and sold it for the astonishing sum of £200,000, which is the equivalent today of over £15,000,000. Now a very rich man, he was able to indulge his passion for travel. As a child he had pored over travel books written by early explorers, and his fancy and imagination had been stirred by family holidays to the sublime mountain regions of Wales and Scotland. 'What lands of spirit-stirring and enriching scenes and places!' he had written. He was to return to these scenes of grandeur in later years to 'recapture the thousands of vivid and tender memories', but with a different purpose. Now in his thirties, and captivated by the new science of photography, Frith set out on a series of pioneering journeys to the Nile regions that occupied him from 1856 until 1860.

INTRIGUE AND ADVENTURE

He took with him on his travels a specially-designed wicker carriage that acted as both dark-room and sleeping chamber. These far-flung journeys were packed with intrigue and adventure. In his life story, written when he was sixty-three, Frith tells of being held captive by bandits, and of fighting 'an awful midnight battle to the very point of surrender with a deadly pack of hungry, wild dogs'. Sporting flowing Arab costume, Frith arrived at Akaba by camel sixty years before Lawrence, where he encountered 'desert princes and rival sheikhs, blazing with jewel-hilted swords'.

During these extraordinary adventures he was assiduously exploring the desert regions bordering the Nile and patiently recording the antiquities and peoples with his camera. He was the first photographer to venture beyond the sixth cataract. Africa was still the mysterious 'Dark Continent', and Stanley and Livingstone's historic meeting was a decade into the future. The conditions for picture taking confound belief. He laboured for hours in his wicker dark-room in the sweltering heat of the desert, while the volatile chemicals fizzed dangerously in their trays. Often he was forced to work in remote tombs and caves

where conditions were cooler. Back in London he exhibited his photographs and was 'rapturously cheered' by members of the Royal Society. His reputation as a photographer was made overnight. An eminent modern historian has likened their impact on the population of the time to that on our own generation of the first photographs taken on the surface of the moon.

VENTURE OF A LIFE-TIME

Characteristically, Frith quickly spotted the opportunity to create a new business as a specialist publisher of photographs. He lived in an era of immense and sometimes violent change. For the poor in the early part of Victoria's reign work was a drudge and the hours long, and people had precious little free time to enjoy themselves.

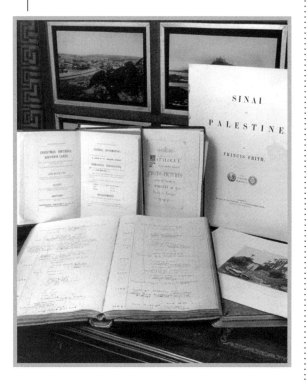

Most had no transport other than a cart or gig at their disposal, and had not travelled far beyond the boundaries of their own town or village. However, by the 1870s, the railways had threaded their way across the country, and Bank Holidays and half-day Saturdays had been made obligatory by Act of Parliament. All of a sudden the ordinary working man and his family were able to enjoy days out and see a little more of the world.

With characteristic business acumen, Francis Frith foresaw that these new tourists would enjoy having souvenirs to commemorate their days out. In 1860 he married Mary Ann Rosling and set out with the intention of photographing every city, town and village in Britain. For the next thirty years he travelled the country by train and by pony and trap, producing fine photographs of seaside resorts and beauty spots that were keenly bought by millions of Victorians. These prints were painstakingly pasted into family albums and pored over during the dark nights of winter, rekindling precious memories of summer excursions.

THE RISE OF FRITH & CO

Frith's studio was soon supplying retail shops all over the country. To meet the demand he gathered about him a small team of photographers, and published the work of independent artist-photographers of the calibre of Roger Fenton and Francis Bedford. In order to gain some understanding of the scale of Frith's business one only has to look at the catalogue issued by Frith & Co in 1886: it runs to some 670

pages, listing not only many thousands of views of the British Isles but also many photographs of most European countries, and China, Japan, the USA and Canada – note the sample page shown above from the hand-written *Frith & Co* ledgers detailing pictures taken. By 1890 Frith had created the greatest specialist photographic publishing company in the world, with over 2,000 outlets – more than the combined number that Boots and WH Smith have today! The picture on the right shows the *Frith & Co* display board at Ingleton in the Yorkshire Dales (left of window). Beautifully constructed with a mahogany frame and gilt inserts, it could display up to a dozen local scenes.

POSTCARD BONANZA

The ever-popular holiday postcard we know today took many years to develop. In 1870 the Post Office issued the first plain cards, with a pre-printed stamp on one face. In 1894 they allowed other publishers' cards to be sent through the mail with an attached adhesive halfpenny stamp. Demand grew rapidly, and in 1895 a new

size of postcard was permitted called the court card, but there was little room for illustration. In 1899, a year after Frith's death, a new card measuring 5.5 x 3.5 inches became the standard format, but it was not until 1902 that the divided back came into being, with address and message on one face and a full-size illustration on the other. *Frith & Co* were in the vanguard of postcard development, and Frith's sons Eustace and Cyril continued their father's monumental task, expanding the number of views offered to the public and recording more and more places in Britain, as the coasts and countryside were opened up to mass travel.

Francis Frith died in 1898 at his villa in Cannes, his great project still growing. The archive he created continued in business for another seventy years. By 1970 it contained over a third of a million pictures of 7,000 cities, towns and villages. The massive photographic record Frith has left to us stands as a living monument to a special and very remarkable man.

Frith's Archive: *A Unique Legacy*

FRANCIS FRITH'S legacy to us today is of immense significance and value, for the magnificent archive of evocative photographs he created provides a unique record of change in 7,000 cities, towns and villages throughout Britain over a century and more. Frith and his fellow studio photographers revisited locations many times down the years to update their views, compiling for us an enthralling and colourful pageant of British life and character.

We tend to think of Frith's sepia views of Britain as nostalgic, for most of us use them to conjure up memories of places in our own lives with which we have family associations. It often makes us forget that to Francis Frith they were records of daily life as it was actually being lived in the cities, towns and villages of his day. The Victorian age was one of great and often bewildering change for ordinary people, and though the pictures evoke an impression of slower times, life was as busy and hectic as it is today.

We are fortunate that Frith was a photographer of the people, dedicated to recording the minutiae of everyday life. For it is this sheer wealth of visual data, the painstaking chronicle of changes in dress, transport, street layouts, buildings, housing, engineering and landscape that captivates us so much today. His remarkable images offer us a powerful link with the past and with the lives of our ancestors.

TODAY'S TECHNOLOGY

Computers have now made it possible for Frith's many thousands of images to be accessed almost instantly. In the Frith archive today, each photograph is carefully 'digitised' then stored on a CD Rom. Frith archivists can locate a single photograph amongst thousands within seconds. Views can be catalogued and sorted under a variety of categories of place and content to the immediate benefit of researchers. Inexpensive reference prints can be created for them at the touch of a mouse button, and a wide range of books and other printed materials assembled and published for a wider, more general readership - in the next twelve months over a hundred Frith local history titles will be published! The

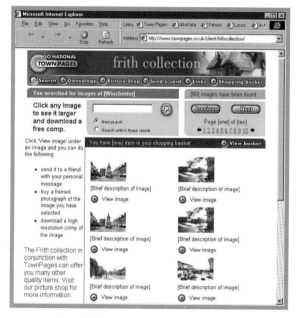

See Frith at www. francisfrith.co.uk

day-to-day workings of the archive are very different from how they were in Francis Frith's time: imagine the herculean task of sorting through eleven tons of glass negatives as Frith had to do to locate a particular sequence of pictures! Yet the archive still prides itself on maintaining the same high standards of excellence laid down by Francis Frith, including the painstaking cataloguing and indexing of every view.

It is curious to reflect on how the internet now allows researchers in America and elsewhere greater instant access to the archive than Frith himself ever enjoyed. Many thousands of individual views can be called up on screen within seconds on one of the Frith internet sites, enabling people living continents away to revisit the streets of their ancestral home town, or view places in Britain where they have enjoyed holidays. Many overseas researchers welcome the chance to view special theme selections, such as transport, sports, costume and ancient monuments.

We are certain that Francis Frith would have heartily approved of these modern developments, for he himself was always working at the very limits of Victorian photographic technology.

THE VALUE OF THE ARCHIVE TODAY

Because of the benefits brought by the computer, Frith's images are increasingly studied by social historians, by researchers into genealogy and ancestory, by architects, town planners, and by teachers and schoolchildren involved in local history projects. In addition, the archive offers every one of us a unique opportunity to examine the places where we and our families have lived and worked down the years. Immensely successful in Frith's own era, the archive is now, a century and more on, entering a new phase of popularity.

THE PAST IN TUNE WITH THE FUTURE

Historians consider the Francis Frith Collection to be of prime national importance. It is the only archive of its kind remaining in private ownership and has been valued at a million pounds. However, this figure is now rapidly increasing as digital technology enables more and more people around the world to enjoy its benefits.

Francis Frith's archive is now housed in an historic timber barn in the beautiful village of Teffont in Wiltshire. Its founder would not recognize the archive office as it is today. In place of the many thousands of dusty boxes containing glass plate negatives and an all-pervading odour of photographic chemicals, there are now ranks of computer screens. He would be amazed to watch his images travelling round the world at unimaginable speeds through network and internet lines.

The archive's future is both bright and exciting. Francis Frith, with his unshakeable belief in making photographs available to the greatest number of people, would undoubtedly approve of what is being done today with his lifetime's work. His photographs, depicting our shared past, are now bringing pleasure and enlightenment to millions around the world a century and more after his death.

HAMPSHIRE – *An Introduction*

FEW COUNTIES in the south of England offer such diversity of scenery and character as Hampshire. Much of it remains unspoilt, and even today it still seems to embody the heart and soul of the English countryside. Stretching from the genteel yachting haven of Lymington in the west to Surrey's manicured commuter belt in the east, it has often been said that Hampshire, one of the larger of the English counties, has something for everyone. With its charming villages, rolling farmland, scenic forests and gentle river valleys, Hampshire's attractions are certainly many and varied. And, of course, there is the county's bracing coastline, littered with monuments to the past and a permanent reminder of how this country has defended itself against attack over the centuries.

Much of the county conveys a sense of space, quiet beauty and dignity in an ever-shrinking world. But what of Hampshire's past? And how much of the county survives intact today? To find the answer, you would need to set off on a journey of discovery in search of the real Hampshire, its spirit and its sense of pride and tradition.

True, some parts of the county have fallen prey to the planner's axe: now, there is little to separate Southampton and Winchester or Fareham and Portsmouth. As the fascinating photographs in this book demonstrate, many old traditions, both in town and country, have been lost and a way of life that we once took for granted but thought would last forever has gradually disappeared. But, though there are constant reminders of the modern world wherever you look, some areas of Hampshire's rural and urban heartland have changed little over the years, retaining their identity and still blessed with a tangible sense of the past. Much has changed and yet much, it seems, has stayed the same.

For example, in the top north-west corner of the county, amid the aptly-named 'Hampshire Highlands', which are probably more commonly known as the North Hampshire Downs, peaceful little villages lie undisturbed in this high downland country; isolated communities that perhaps not surprisingly have changed little over the centuries.

The river valleys and water meadows of mid and south Hampshire are some of the finest in the country - the sparkling waters of the Hamble, Anton, Itchen, Meon and Test adding an extra touch of beauty to their surroundings. Many of the photographs depicting these rivers have a timeless quality about them. The towns of Andover, Romsey and Petersfield may have expanded over the years but their bustling, colourful market squares survive, evoking images of how traditional country towns used to be. Compare some of the photographs in this book with the reality and you will see how little these town centres have changed in the last 100 years or so.

Winchester, at the heart of Hampshire and the 12th century, concealed in a coffin! Walter Raleigh was condemned to death in Winchester in 1603, and Judge Jeffreys held his bloody assizes here in 1685. There are many fine buildings within the city boundaries but the pride of Winchester, of course, is its magnificent, world-famous Cathedral.

Further south lies the New Forest, the jewel in Hampshire's crown. The largest remaining unspoilt medieval forest in Western Europe and once a royal preserve, it is a romantic place of dark legends and historic literary associations. The forest, which

once the capital of England, recalls the past at every turn and round each corner. No visit to the county is complete without a tour of this most historic of English cities. Winchester was an important centre from Roman times when it was known as Venta Belgarum. Later, it became the capital of England and Wessex under the Anglo Saxons. William the Conqueror retained Winchester as his capital and built a castle here, though much of it was destroyed during the Civil War. However, the Great Hall still survives and can be visited. Empress Matilda escaped from the castle in extends roughly from the south coast to the Wiltshire border, conjures up images of wild, uncultivated tracts of land and extensive dense woodland. In medieval times that is precisely how the New Forest was made up. Today, apart from obvious signs of commercialism, the forest has changed little since William the Conqueror established it as his deer park. The two main towns in the region, Lyndhurst and Brockenhurst, developed during the 19th century and prospered even more in the 20th century, largely as a result of increased tourism. But it is not just the New

Forest that boasts such extensive tree cover. There are other lesser-known forests and extensive areas of woodland within Hampshire's boundaries. For example, the ancient Forest of Bere once covered a band of countryside from Southampton to the Sussex border. In the 11th century it was designated a Royal Forest by William the Conqueror, though little of it remains today apart from occasional patches of woodland. Much of the forest was cleared to provide oak timber for the building of Tudor warships, and the villages of Bucklers Hard and Bursledon recall the days when those great vessels were built on their slipways. The Alice Holt Forest, adjacent to the Surrey border, and the Queen Elizabeth Country Park, north of Portsmouth, are popular amenity areas with many attractions for walkers and cyclists.

And so we come to the port of Southampton and Hampshire's historic coastline. Acting as a symbolic gateway to the world, Southampton Water is the wide estuary of two great rivers - the Test and the Itchen. In the golden days of ocean-going travel, this internationally famous waterway provided first-time visitors to these shores with one of the first glimpses of English soil. Today, the waterfront is more heavily industrialised and the great passenger liners are certainly fewer. But the sense of maritime history is still tangible as one recalls the names of the great, majestic liners which once plied these historic waters - the 'Mauretania', the 'Aquitania', the 'Queen Mary' and 'Queen Elizabeth' among them. The ill-fated 'Titanic' sailed from Southampton in 1912, and the 'Great Eastern' was moored in Southampton Water prior to her maiden voyage in 1861. Southampton Water has also played a key role in the development of flying boats and seaplanes, which is superbly illustrated in the city's Hall of Aviation. Today, the scene is still a bustling one - you do not have to wait long before you spot an oil tanker, a tug or a ferry, and the low roar of the sleek hydrofoil may arouse your interest as it zips in and out of Southampton Docks.

There is always something worth seeing on Southampton Water, and never far from view

is the splendid green dome of the chapel at Netley, all that remains of the Royal Victoria Military Hospital. Following reports of the dreadful conditions in the Crimea, it was Queen Victoria who argued the need for such a hospital, its objective to care for the sick and injured casualties of war. Of the 54,000 troops despatched in that bloody battle, 9,000 came back as war-weary invalids, while nearly 20,000 perished. The 220-acre site at Netley was purchased in 1856, and in May that year Queen Victoria laid the foundation stone beneath which lay a prototype of the newly instituted Victoria Cross decoration and a Crimea medal. The building attracted criticism - John Wise, the historian, dismissed its distinctive appearance by saying 'the new government hospital loads the shore with all its costly ugliness'. Florence Nightingale did not endorse the hospital's elaborate design either; she was particularly incensed by its anomalous layout, with some wards facing the sunless north. Though Netley was completed too late to play a role in the Crimea, for the next 100 years it contributed to the medical welfare of thousands of fighting men on active service throughout the world.

The shores of Southampton Water conceal hidden pockets of unspoilt countryside and commonland, and here and there one can stumble on picturesque creeks and attractive woodland. Mostly, though, this part of Hampshire has gradually been swallowed up by urban and residential development over the years; further along the coast, to the east of Southampton Water, the ribbon of towns and villages lies in the shadow of Portsmouth, described in ancient times as 'the glory and the bulwark of these ancient kingdoms'. From Portsdown Hill, which rises above the city,

there are impressive views over a vast concrete jungle stretching to the sea. At the western end of the hill stands the Nelson monument, a local landmark. This one, built in 1807, is not as imposing as the monument in London, but the inscription reads 'Consecrated to the memory of Lord Viscount Nelson by the zealous attachment of those who fought at Trafalgar to perpetuate his triumph and their regret'. The monument looks out over Portsmouth, Britain's only island city, towards Nelson's great flagship HMS 'Victory', which sailed from here for the last time in 1805.

It was a royal commission in 1860 which recommended that this area be better defended in order to avoid enemy forces from taking the hill. The Cabinet was split over the idea, and Gladstone, Chancellor at the time, threatened to resign. However, Palmerston was not easily swayed in such matters, advising Queen Victoria that 'it was better to lose Gladstone than to lose Portsmouth'. Work on six polygonal forts on Portsdown Hill went ahead, though we may be thankful that they were never put to use. The low position of the forts and the way they so easily blended into the contours of the hill meant that from the north they were hardly visible at all. This was a deliberate ploy to deceive the enemy, should the French come ashore along the Sussex coast and then try to make an assault on Portsmouth from the rear.

Richard I established a settlement on Portsea Island and it was he who built the first dock at Portsmouth in the late 12th century. The Tudor Kings, Henry VII and Henry VIII, later constructed the first dry dock in the world here. So, from its early beginnings, Portsmouth evolved over the years into the south of England's largest and most important naval base. During the Second World War, Portsmouth was heavily bombed, suffering more than 60 aerial bombardments. The Guildhall was badly damaged by fire and the shops in the High Street were decimated.

North of Portsmouth, the countryside is surprisingly pretty and unspoiled. The quiet woodland paths and rural byways have changed little since the final preparations were made hereabouts for the planned invasion of Europe on 6th June 1944. It was at Southwick House, now virtually engulfed by the buildings of the naval establishment, that Supreme Commander General Dwight Eisenhower and the Chiefs of Staff gathered to mastermind the huge operation. The operation room with its board used to plot the progress of Operation Overlord is still intact.

Further north is the town of Petersfield. Nearby is the Shoulder of Mutton Hill, setting for the Poet Stone, a sarsen stone dedicated to the memory of the Edwardian poet Edward Thomas who was killed in the First World War. Thomas lived in the area, and it was his deep and abiding love for the beech hangers and the distant downland glimpses that so inspired him in his writing. Unveiling the monument, Walter de la Mare commented 'when he (Thomas) was killed in Flanders, a mirror of England was shattered'. The theme of defence is evident once more in Hampshire's north-east corner. Here is Farnborough, synonymous with aviation, while next door is Aldershot, long renowned as the home of the British Army.

We may be thankful that the spirit of Hampshire, so evident in these illustrations, lives on today. Much of our world may have changed for good, but Francis Frith's photographs of the county evoke special memories that will never die.

ABBOTTS ANN, THE VILLAGE c1955 A4004
Abbotts Ann takes its name from the Pillhill brook, originally the Anna or Ann stream. The manor was granted to New Minster, later Hyde Abbey, at Winchester in 901, and the village subsequently became known as Abbotts Ann.

ABBOTTS ANN, THE VILLAGE 1898 42093

In the early 18th century the manor passed to Thomas Pitt, an enterprising businessman who made a lot of money by selling a valuable diamond to the Regent of France. He became known as 'Diamond' Pitt and, having made a profit of £100,000 on the sale, he rebuilt the village church in 1716.

AMPORT, THE VILLAGE 1898 42092

During the 1830s this pretty village was the scene of a major uprising among farm labourers, with angry mobs burning hayricks and destroying machinery. The workers were demanding a rise from 8s to 12s per week and although most of them got what they wanted, by 1846 the average weekly local wage was back to 8s.

UPPER CLATFORD
The Village **1899** 43693
The village lies at the confluence of the River Anton
and the Pillhill brook. The name Clatford means 'ford
where burdock grew'. 30 years before this picture was
taken, the first locally manufactured traction engine
trundled through the village on its way to the Royal
Agricultural Show at Southampton.

UPPER CLATFORD, FISHING COTTAGE c1955 U53001

UPPER CLATFORD
Fishing Cottage c1955
The picturesque Anton flowing through Upper Clatford. Partially visible, on the left of the photograph, in a meadow fed by the river, is the little church. Near the village are the remains of a sizeable Iron Age hill-fort.

◆

WHERWELL
The Village 1901
Wherwell is famous for its ruined priory, established by the Saxon Queen Elfreda, mother of Ethelred the Unready, possibly as an act of repentance following several dark deeds. Some sources suggest that, during the Civil War, shots fired by Cromwell's cannon at Wherwell Priory inadvertently hit the door of the local pub.

WHERWELL, THE VILLAGE 1901 46353

ANDOVER, THE TOWN HALL 1898 42081
The Town Hall dates back to 1826; the building's Greek Doric style makes it one of Andover's most distinguished landmarks. Either side of the market place in front of it are various 19th century buildings, some of which were quite new when this photograph was taken.

ANDOVER, DISTANT PROSPECT 1899 43689
The name of the town was first recorded in AD 955 as Andeferas. Andover was a municipal borough as long ago as the reign of King John, and later became an established centre for the wool trade. Various Iron Age sites and encampments illustrate the area's wealth of history.

ANDOVER
Bridge Street **1901** 46347
The Cyclists Touring Club sign can be seen on the facade of the White Hart Commercial Hotel on the left of this photograph. On the right is the early 19th century Star and Garter, which later became the Danebury Hotel. Note the sizeable Tuscan porch.

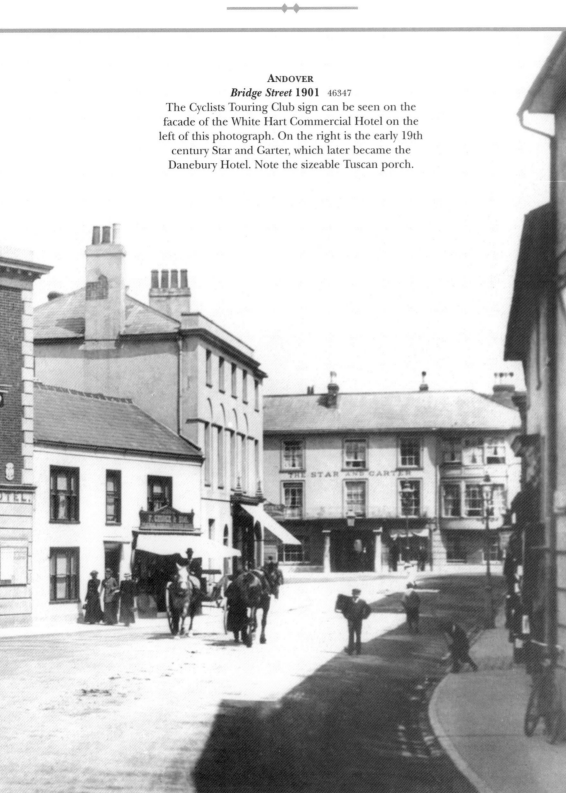

ANDOVER
High Street **1908** 60092
Medieval Andover was established around a market which
stands in the shadow of the 19th century church of St Mary,
built in the Early English style by a former headmaster of
Winchester College and described as the best Victorian church
in Hampshire. However, an author said of the town in 1908
'little else than tradition remains of old Andover'.

ANDOVER, ANTON MILL 1906 54631

ANDOVER
Anton Mill 1906
A child gazes wistfully into the tranquil waters of the River Anton, a tributary of the Test, which rises to the north of Andover and runs through the heart of the town. The river has witnessed thousands of years of history; the people of the Stone Age made their homes on its banks.

ANNA VALLEY
Little Ann Village c1955
Ann or Anna was originally the name for the shining stream now known as the Pillhill Brook, a tributary of the River Anton. To the north-west lies Weyhill, famous for its large country fair dating back to the 13th century.

ANNA VALLEY, LITTLE ANN VILLAGE c1955 A53006

ROMSEY, SADLER'S MILL c1955 R53026
It was wool and brewing that put Romsey on the map; several mills were established on the picturesque streams and watercourses of the River Test, which is fed by clear springs under the chalk soil and has long been renowned for its trout fishing.

ROMSEY, GENERAL VIEW 1920 85038
The town of Romsey is known for its associations with two distinguished Englishmen. Admiral of the Fleet Earl Mountbatten of Burma and Lord Palmerston, Conservative Prime Minister during Queen Victoria's reign, both lived here. The town's War Memorial Park includes a 150-mm Japanese gun captured in Burma at the end of World War Two.

ROMSEY, BROADLANDS 1898 42110
Situated to the south of the town, overlooking the Test, Broadlands is an imposing porticoed house remodelled in classical style by 'Capability' Brown and John Holland in the mid 18th century. Lord Palmerston was born here, and his favourite room looks out over the river.

ROMSEY, THE HUNDRED 1911 63781

The Hundred, which runs down to the Market Place, is lined with striking houses and cottages. The Sawyers Arms, now a private house, can be spotted on the right. A few doors along, a large enamel Nestles sign is just visible.

ROMSEY, THE ABBEY 1898 42098

The great Norman church is one of the most impressive in Europe and certainly the finest in Hampshire. The abbey was founded in AD 907 by Edward the Elder, son of Alfred the Great, but the main part of the building was built in the 12th century by Henry de Blois, Bishop of Winchester.

ROMSEY
Market Place **1904** 51431
The imposing figure of Lord Palmerston surveys
Romsey's Market Place. The market town became a
borough in 1607 and since then it has had five town
halls, including the Guildhall, which is now a pub, the
Tudor Rose.

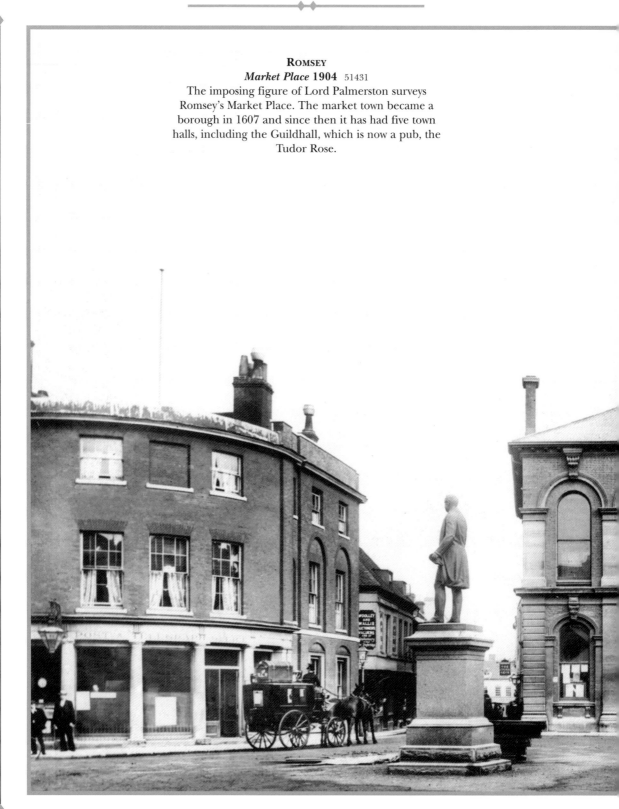

ROMSEY, OLD CORN EXCHANGE 1932 85040

To the right of Romsey's Corn Exchange, built in 1864, is a glimpse of Romsey Abbey, which until the mid 16th century was home to a Benedictine order of nuns. At the time of the Dissolution, the abbey was saved from destruction by the people of Romsey who paid £100 for it.

CADNAM, SIR JOHN BARLEYCORN 1932 85062

A Hants & Dorset bus approaching the Sir John Barleycorn pub at Cadnam in the New Forest. This thatched building was once owned by Strong's, the Romsey-based brewery which was leased to Thomas Strong in 1858. Whitbread acquired Strong's in 1969 and brewing ceased in 1981.v

EMERY DOWN 1904 51463
Half a mile from Lyndhurst and yet located within the parish lies the scattered hamlet of Emery Down, surrounded by peaceful forest glades and countryside. This settlement was once a centre for smuggling, a flourishing local industry that continued until the turn of the century, just before this photograph was taken.

LYNDHURST
High Street **1908** 60106
Note the hay rake, coal-scuttles and assortment of piping and rope adorning the window of the local ironmongers in the centre of Lyndhurst. Next to it is John Strange, the butchers, and opposite are the premises of Misselbrook & West, their window advertising New Zealand lamb - 'choicest quality from the world's finest pastures'.

BURLEY, THE CROSS AND POST OFFICE c1960 B647032
A penny-farthing can be seen leaning against the front of the cycle stores in the centre of Burley, which John Wise described in 1863 as 'one of the most primitive of (New) Forest hamlets'. By the time this photograph was taken, approximately one hundred years later, it was firmly on the tourist trail.

LYMINGTON, THE HIGH STREET FROM THE CHURCH 1958 L148142
An important sailing centre, Lymington was originally a Saxon port with shipbuilding in operation between the Norman era and the 18th century. This photograph of the town was taken from the tower of St Thomas's church at the top of the High Street, depicting an elegant mix of Georgian houses, bow-fronted cottages and covered shop fronts.

BUCKLERS HARD
The Village c1960 B43024

One of the New Forest's most famous landmarks, Bucklers Hard was an important naval shipbuilding yard during the 18th century. The tiny settlement of picturesque cottages looking down towards the Beaulieu River has hardly changed at all since the most famous ship built at Bucklers Hard, Nelson's 'Agamemnon', was launched here in 1781.

◆

BEAULIEU
The Abbey 1908 60484

Founded as a Cistercian abbey by King John in 1204, Beaulieu is Norman French for 'beautiful place'. Much of the building was destroyed at the Dissolution and many of the stones removed to other sites. This photograph depicts the magnificent ruins of the abbey in their timeless setting.

BUCKLERS HARD, THE VILLAGE c1960 B43024

BEAULIEU, THE ABBEY 1908 60484

BROCKENHURST, THE VILLAGE c1955 B394006

The name Brockenhurst means 'the badger's wood'. The local churchyard includes a famous, intricately carved monument to 'Brusher' Mills, a renowned local snake catcher who died about 50 years before this photograph was taken. He earned his nickname by sweeping loose snow off the ice on Brockenhurst pond to make it easier for skaters.

BROCKENHURST, THE CROSSING c1955 B394008

Thanks to a railway station providing train services to London, Brockenhurst began to expand during the second half of the 19th century and continued to develop in the 20th century, establishing itself as a convenient and popular inland resort within the boundaries of the New Forest.

BRANSGORE
The Post Office c1960

Bransgore, north of Christchurch, grew over the years as a sprawling residential village. Bournville Cocoa can be seen advertised in the window of the local post office and stores - a reminder of the days when the village shop was an integral part of the community.

◆

RINGWOOD
Avon Castle 1891

This late 19th-century mock castle was built 'at great cost and with the best materials and workmanship' by John Turner Turner, a renowned sportsman and big game hunter. With its 13-acre grounds and Avon river frontage, the castle became a popular weekend retreat for Turner Turner's many friends. There was even a chapel and a private railway halt.

BRANSGORE, THE POST OFFICE c1960 B695001

RINGWOOD, AVON CASTLE 1891 28650

RINGWOOD
The Millstream **1900** 45027
This turn of the century photograph shows a thatcher
busy at work on the roof of a picturesque cottage on
the banks of the River Avon, which flows serenely
through Ringwood on its way to Christchurch and the
sea. Peeping above the trees is the parish church,
rebuilt during the 19th century.

CHILWORTH, THE VILLAGE 1906 53379

Children at play in the village of Chilworth, outside Southampton. One of Chilworth's buildings, originally designed to house the squire's hounds, became the village post office six years before this photograph was taken. One hundred years earlier, the church was described as 'little better than a hovel, with a belfry like a pigeon-house', though its 12th-century bells were among the oldest in Hampshire.

SOUTHAMPTON, ROYAL PIER PAVILION 1908 60415

The Royal Pier, at the eastern end of Mayflower Park, was opened in 1833 and for many years was the largest in the south of England. The pier was reconstructed during the early 1890s and the pavilion's distinctive onion domes added in the late 1920s.

SOUTHAMPTON, HIGH STREET 1908 60418

Many of the buildings in Southampton's historic High Street were destroyed during the Second World War, more than 30 years after this photograph was taken. Horse-drawn trams were introduced in 1879 and electrified in 1900. Over on the left, near Liptons, is Below Bar Post Office.

SOUTHAMPTON, THE BARGATE 1908 60428

One of the finest medieval gateways in the country, Southampton's Bargate dates back to the late 12th century. Up until the 1930s specially designed trams travelled through Bargate, with dome-shaped tops to fit the arch. The adjoining walls and buildings were subsequently destroyed so that traffic bypassed Bargate.

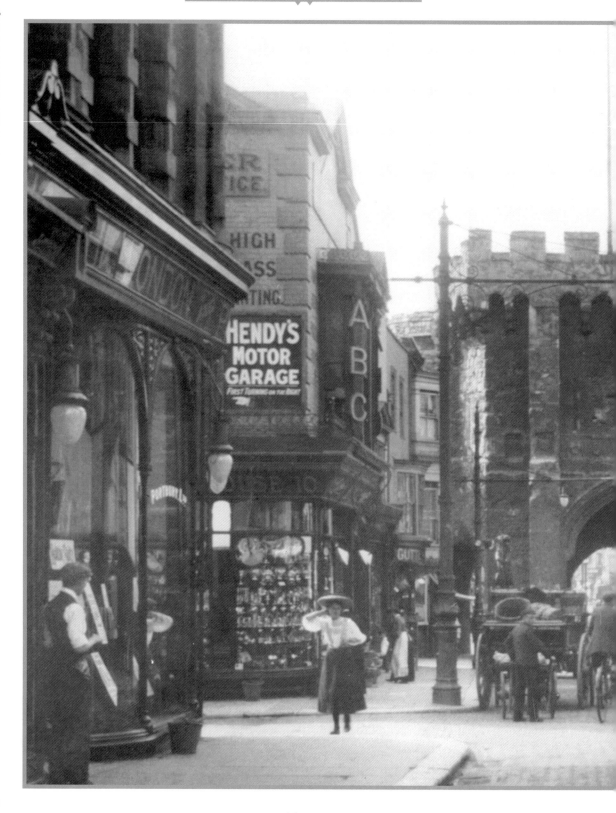

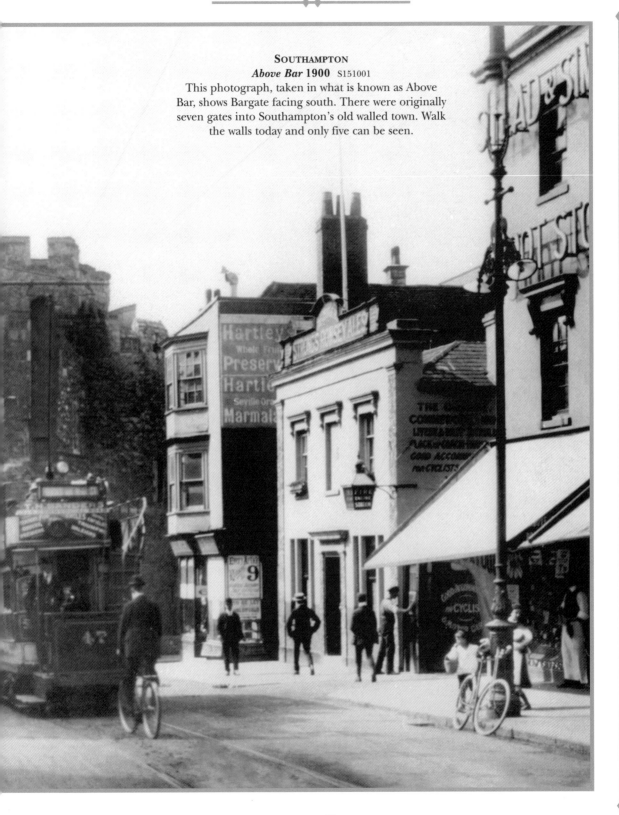

SOUTHAMPTON
Above Bar **1900** S151001
This photograph, taken in what is known as Above
Bar, shows Bargate facing south. There were originally
seven gates into Southampton's old walled town. Walk
the walls today and only five can be seen.

SOUTHAMPTON, FLOOD GATE BAR 1892 31334

SOUTHAMPTON
Flood Gate Bar **1892**
On the right of the picture is the 15th-century God's House Tower, formerly the south-east gate of the old town and one of the earliest artillery fortifications in Europe. A ditch ran alongside the building until the 1850s, intended to link Southampton with the Andover Canal and the River Test.

◆

SOUTHAMPTON
In Dry Dock **1908**
The 'Finland' in Number 6 Dry Dock in Southampton. The vessel was not a regular visitor to the port and could have been here on charter. Southampton's other main dry dock, Trafalgar, was opened in 1905 and probably would have been used by the 'Titanic' had she survived.

SOUTHAMPTON, IN DRY DOCK 1908 60442

WOOLSTON, THE FLOATING BRIDGE c1955 W468003

Southampton's famous Floating Bridge enabled foot passengers and traffic to cross the Itchen between the city and the south-eastern suburb of Woolston. The steam-powered floating bridge was in service for 141 years, between 1836 and 1977. A high-level road bridge eventually replaced it.

NETLEY, THE ABBEY 1908 60467

Founded in 1239 by the monks of Beaulieu Abbey, Netley Abbey occupies a pretty, wooded setting close to Southampton Water. The abbey was dissolved in 1536 and later became a private mansion. In the 18th century it passed to a Southampton builder who was killed by falling tracery as he began to demolish the site.

NETLEY, THE HOSPITAL FROM THE PIER 1908 60464
Netley Hospital, which opened in 1868, was a quarter of a mile long and cost more than £300,000 to construct. The sick, dying and injured were brought from the war-torn corners of the British Empire and the 570ft-long pier enabled casualties to be carried ashore from the troop ships. The hospital was demolished in 1966.

BOTLEY, THE MARKET HALL C1955 B544027

The 19th-century radical farmer and journalist William Cobbett lived in Botley and described it as 'the most delightful village in the world'. This photograph shows the Dolphin Hotel on the right of the square, next to the mid 19th-century Market Hall. At one time Botley boasted fourteen inns.

BOTLEY, THE STATION C1960 B544059

A memorial stone at the entrance to Botley station recalls the murder in 1800 of one Thomas Webb. The killer, a soldier from Botley barracks, was convicted of murder and subsequently executed, his body hanging from a gibbet on Curdridge Common.

BOTLEY
Hambledon Hounds c1960 B544301

The hunt assembling at the front of the Bugle pub, a former coaching inn. Note the sturdy porch, similar to that of its opposite neighbour the Dolphin Hotel. Botley, once a small inland port, stands at the head of navigation on the River Hamble, and barges travelled upstream for corn, coal and timber until the early 20th century.

BOTLEY, THE MILLS C1950 B544006

This picture, showing the 18th-century mill facade, was taken shortly before the construction of a silo block used for storing raw materials for making animal feeds. The new building stands at the right hand end of the flour mill, which is mentioned in the Domesday Book. Some of the silo sections can be seen at the edge of the wharf.

EASTLEIGH, MARKET STREET C1955 E167001

Originally a village, Eastleigh expanded rapidly around Bishopstoke Junction after the London and South Western Railway Company's carriage works moved here in 1889-90, followed by the locomotive workshops in 1909. Much of the town dates from between 1890 and 1939, and many of its residents were employed by the railway.

EASTLEIGH, SOUTHAMPTON AIRPORT C1960 E167030
Southampton Airport lies to the south of Eastleigh town centre and it was from here that the first Spitfire began her maiden flight in 1936. Many of the old buildings seen here have gone, replaced by an airport complex designed to meet the needs of the modern age.

BISHOPSTOKE, THE VILLAGE C1955 B693006
Here we see the River Itchen flowing through Bishopstoke. In 1838, the writer Robert Maudie observed: 'church and the village are beautifully situated, the former close by the bank of the river'. In 1908 another historian recorded that 'many modern red-brick cottages are now in process of building to supply the needs of the men who are employed in the Eastleigh Railway Works'.

TWYFORD, 1000-YEAR-OLD YEW TREE C1955 T284004

The mighty yew tree in Twyford churchyard has a 15-ft circumference and is thought to be the oldest clipped yew in the country. The American statesman Benjamin Franklin wrote part of his autobiography while staying in Twyford, and the young Alexander Pope was expelled from school here for taunting his tutor in satirical verse.

WINCHESTER, GENERAL PROSPECT 1893 32648

A brisk climb above Winchester is always well rewarded by the beautiful views of the city, its handsome and historic buildings clustered round the hollow in which this one-time capital of England sits. To the right of the cathedral is Winchester's 19th-century Guildhall, its bracket clock made by a local craftsman.

WINCHESTER, HIGH STREET 1896 37243
Winchester's High Street boasts a variety of Georgian, Victorian and half-timbered Elizabethan buildings; some of them still have their original shop fronts and doorways. Just off the High Street is Jewry Street, a part of the city once populated by Jewish traders and moneylenders.

WINCHESTER, HIGH STREET 1928 80887
Policemen directing traffic at the top of the High Street in this late 1920s photograph. The George Hotel, on the left, was demolished in the 1950s to facilitate a road-widening scheme. Replicas of two High Street shops, a chemist and a tobacconist, can be seen in the City Museum.

WINCHESTER
Butter Cross **1899** 43677
The restored medieval Butter Cross, or High Cross,
marks the site of a market. The town crier has long
stood on this spot in order to communicate important
news to the people of Winchester. The nearby
pillar-box stands near the site of the old town pump.

WINCHESTER
St Giles Hill **1899** 42968
This photograph was taken 2 years before the famous
statue of King Alfred was erected in the middle of the
road, commemorating the 1000th anniversary of his
death - albeit belatedly, as he died in AD 899! The fair
on St Giles Hill was one of the largest in Europe,
attracting many traders.

WINCHESTER, THE CATHEDRAL 1886 19407
Founded in 1079 and consecrated in 1093, Winchester Cathedral has a vast number of treasures stored within it.
Many distinguished figures lie buried here - among them Jane Austen and Izaak Walton. The cathedral also
includes the tomb of King William Rufus, who was killed by an arrow in the nearby New Forest in 1100.

WINCHESTER, THE CATHEDRAL 1911 63722

WINCHESTER
The Cathedral **1911**

The west door of Winchester Cathedral - one of the city's most famous views. Inside is the stunning 12th-century black marble font from Tournai in Belgium. There are also some magnificent 14th-century carved stalls, a beautiful 15th-century reredos and older coffers containing the bones of Saxon and Danish Kings.

◆

WINCHESTER
Queen Mary's Chair **1911**

Mary I married Prince Philip of Spain in Winchester Cathedral on 25 July 1554 and this chair, upholstered in blue velvet, was used by the Queen during the ceremony. Tapestries completed in Flanders decorated the nave for the occasion.

WINCHESTER, QUEEN MARY'S CHAIR 1911 63730

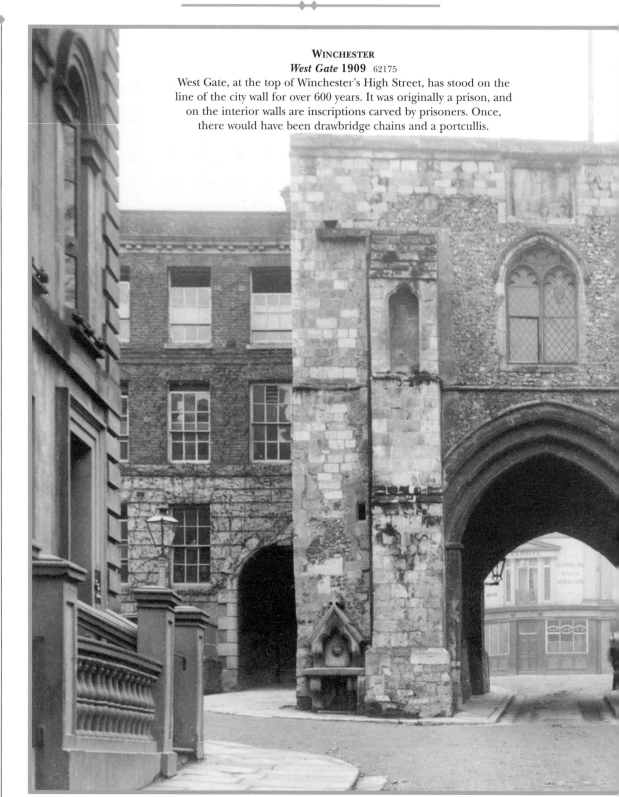

WINCHESTER
West Gate **1909** 62175

West Gate, at the top of Winchester's High Street, has stood on the
line of the city wall for over 600 years. It was originally a prison, and
on the interior walls are inscriptions carved by prisoners. Once,
there would have been drawbridge chains and a portcullis.

WINCHESTER, FROM WEST GATE 1923 74230
The city as seen from the West Gate. On the right are the offices of the Hampshire Advertiser, and in the distance is the old Guildhall from where a curfew bell is rung every evening at 8.00.

WINCHESTER, THE BARRACKS C1960 W107111
The former Peninsula Barracks stand on the site of a medieval castle which was destroyed after the Civil War. The land was acquired by Charles II, who commissioned Christopher Wren to build a palace in place of the castle. The palace was never finished and burnt to the ground in 1894.

WINCHESTER, THE GREAT HALL 1912 64458

Considered to be the best medieval hall in the country after Westminster Hall, the Great Hall dates back to the early 13th century and includes fine arcade piers of Purbeck marble. The Round Table, traditionally associated with King Arthur, can be seen hanging on the west wall.

WINCHESTER, ST CROSS CHURCH 1906 55879

The splendid church of St Cross was built between 1170 and 1230 for the poor brethren and is a fine architectural mix of Norman and Early English. The squat tower is thought to have been rebuilt in 1384. Inside, there is a striking Norman font and a lectern of 1509.

WINCHESTER, ST CROSS CHURCH 1919 68966
An interesting view of the church of St Cross from the porter's lodge, where a visitor can be seen receiving the traditional 'Wayfarer's Dole' of bread and ale. Note the sign on the wall: 'Tickets to view the church and hospital can be obtained here - Sundays excepting'.

WINCHESTER, ST CROSS HOSPITAL 1906 55884
The Hospital of St Cross was founded by Bishop Henry de Blois in 1136 and is the oldest almshouse in England, originally built to house, clothe and feed 'thirteen poor impotent men, so reduced in strength as rarely or never to be able to raise themselves without the assistance of another'.

BISHOP'S WALTHAM, HIGH STREET c1955 B612002
Bishop's Waltham is still remembered for having the only privately owned bank in the country, before it was sold to Barclays in the early 1950s. The Bishop's Waltham and Hampshire Bank was founded in 1809 and was later known as Gunner's Bank.

BISHOP'S WALTHAM, THE VILLAGE c1955 B612006

DROXFORD, THE MILL c1960 D198012

BISHOP'S WALTHAM
The Village c1955

The centre of Bishop's Waltham has retained its character over the years, and this photograph shows some of the country town's striking Georgian buildings. Bishop's Waltham is famous for its ruined palace, built by Bishop Henry de Blois around 1135. William of Wykeham died here in 1404.

◆

DROXFORD
The Mill c1960

Izaak Walton fished here in the Meon, reflecting that the valley 'exceeds all England for swift, shallow, clear, pleasant brooks and store of trout'. Churchill, the War Cabinet and the Allied Chiefs used the local railway station as their headquarters during the planning of D-Day in 1944, conducting operations in a special train based here.

WICKHAM, CHESAPEAKE MILL c1965 W491047

Chesapeake Mill dates back to 1820 and was built by John Prior, a miller, partly of woodwork from an American warship of that name, captured by the much smaller British HMS 'Shannon' off Boston Harbour in 1813. It was later auctioned at Portsmouth and broken up.

BURSLEDON, THE BRIDGE c1955 B304008

Between the 14th and early 19th centuries, Bursledon was an important centre for naval shipbuilding, with the wooded slopes of the River Hamble providing much of the timber. HMS 'Elephant', Nelson's 74-gun flagship at the Battle of Copenhagen, was built here by George Parsons and launched at his yard in 1786.

BURSLEDON, THE VILLAGE c1960 B304003

Bursledon is divided into two distinct halves - the new and the old. The older part is naturally more interesting, with its quaint old buildings clinging to the banks of the Hamble. Visitors to Bursledon often recall the little Gothic belfry at the entrance to the Roman Catholic Chapel of Our Lady of the Rosary.

FAREHAM, WEST STREET c1955 F103014

On the left can be seen the Embassy Cinema, which at the time this photograph was taken was showing 'The African Queen' with Humphrey Bogart. Further down are Woolworth's and Dewhurst Butchers. West Street is the commercial heart of Fareham, described by Thackeray, who spent his school holidays here, as 'a dear little old Hampshire town'.

LEE-ON-THE-SOLENT, LEE TOWER FROM THE WEST c1955 L461011
Lee-on-the-Solent grew as a late-Victorian development. Its railway and pier, both now gone, prompted ambitious plans to transform the town into a major seaside resort similar in size to Brighton or Bournemouth, but the scheme failed to make the grade. The 120-ft tower seen here was demolished in 1969.

GOSPORT, THORNGATE HALL 1898 42720
Built in the 1880s as a memorial to William Thorngate, a philanthropic grocer and tea merchant who donated money for local housing, the Thorngate Hall was regularly used for public meetings until it was gutted by an incendiary bomb in the winter of 1940. It was demolished in the 1950s and replaced with a new building.

ALVERSTOKE, THE CRESCENT 1898 42722

This handsome crescent dates back to 1826 and was originally intended to be part of a seaside resort known as Anglesey, developed by the Marquis of Anglesey. Note the Anglesey Family Hotel on the right. Various other 19th-century buildings survive, but the ambitious scheme never reached fruition and Alverstoke, once a small village on the Haslar Creek, was eventually swallowed up by Gosport.

STOKES BAY, THE BEACH 1898 42727

Just a handful of people and two bathing machines can be seen in this late-Victorian photograph of Stokes Bay. Having travelled by train from London to Gosport, it was from here that Queen Victoria used to set sail for Osborne House, her beloved summer home on the Isle of Wight.

DRAYTON, HAVANT ROAD c1955 D224022

Drayton, a suburb of Portsmouth, lies close to Portsdown Hill, a 7-mile chalk ridge stretching from Bedhampton to Fareham. Apart from its importance in terms of fortification, Portsdown Hill was also a vital link in communication, enabling signals to be transmitted between Whitehall and the fleet at Portsmouth.

PORTCHESTER, THE CASTLE 1892 30030A

Portchester Castle was built by the Romans to defend the English Channel from raiding Saxons and is one of the largest of the 'Saxon shore' forts. Located on a spit overlooking Portsmouth Harbour, the castle was regularly used by kings when visiting Portsmouth. Henry VIII came here with Anne Boleyn.

PORTSMOUTH
Guildhall Square **1892** 30002
Portsmouth's magnificent Guildhall, one of
Hampshire's stateliest civic buildings, was opened in
1890 by the Prince of Wales on behalf of his mother
Queen Victoria who was said to be alarmed by the
endless number of steps leading up to its grand
entrance. The sign on the right advertises 'Town Hall
Concerts every Saturday at 7.30'.

PORTSMOUTH
The Harbour **1892** 30004
Richard I was responsible for establishing a settlement
on Portsea Island, and it was he who built the first
dock at Portsmouth in the late 12th century. The
Tudor kings, Henry VII and VIII, later constructed the
first dry dock in the world here.

PORTSMOUTH, THE HARBOUR AND HMS 'VICTORY' 1890 22754

A considerable amount of development took place here in the 17th and 18th centuries, including the building of naval establishments and factories. Most of the dockyard, where Nelson's flagship HMS 'Victory' has remained more or less intact since the Battle of Trafalgar, also dates from around that time.

PORTSMOUTH, THE HARD 1890 22751

This photograph of The Hard, overlooking Portsmouth Harbour, shows at least three pubs - including The Victoria and Albert in the centre of the picture. The many waterfront drinking houses would have tempted Portsmouth's shifting population of sailors. On the extreme right are the premises of the now defunct National Provincial Bank of England.

PORTSMOUTH, THE ARTIST CORNER, SALLY PORT c1955 P100065
Outside the city walls and isolated from the rest of Portsmouth, Spice Island was once filled with sailors and press gangs. The Round Tower and neighbouring Square Tower squat on the old curtain wall, acting as a permanent reminder of the city's need to defend itself from enemy attack. To the right lies Broad Street.

SOUTHSEA, SALLY PORT c1965 S161113
200 years ago convicts departed from here, en route to Australia, while for many naval officers and British monarchs, this famous gateway represented one of their last views of England before setting off to some distant corner of the world. HMS 'Dolphin' can be seen across the water at Haslar.

SOUTHSEA, THE PROMENADE 1892 30021

SOUTHSEA, THE PARADE 1890 22771

SOUTHSEA
The Promenade **1892**
It was one man, Thomas Owen, a land and property speculator, who developed this part of Portsea Island, transforming it into a residential suburb of Portsmouth. Southsea was initially populated by dockyard workers and retired people.

◆

SOUTHSEA
The Parade **1890**
Southsea started life as a group of farm cottages but by the time this photograph was taken, it bore the stamp of a classic seaside resort, characterised by the terraces, villas and open spaces so typical of coastal towns.

SOUTHSEA, THE PIER 1892 30029

Southsea's pier is strewn with advertising slogans. Sunlight Soap signs adorn the pier structure, while to the right of them a sign advertises 500 perambulators for hire.

SOUTHSEA, THE BEACH 1892 30017

Busy with vendors and visitors and strewn with small boats and sailing craft, Southsea's beach is alive with activity in this Victorian photograph. Long ago, this part of the Hampshire coast consisted of marsh and sandy wastes; it was from here that Henry III amassed his armies to re-conquer France.

Southsea

***The Beach and Pier* 1898** 42693

Southsea's long shingle beach crowded with trippers.
Not surprisingly, everyone in the picture is fully
dressed. During the prim Victorian era, to discard
even one item of clothing would have been unthink-
able. Despite the shingle, patches of sand uncovered
at low tide made the beach a popular attraction.

SOUTHSEA
Dagmar Terrace **1890** 22764
It was during the Victorian era that Southsea established itself as a fashionable holiday resort for the middle classes. Many large hotels were built at this time
and by 1900 all available land had been used
for building.

SOUTHSEA, THE SANDS AND PIER 1921 71472

SOUTHSEA
The Sands and Pier 1921
Southsea is not without its literary associations. H.G.Wells and Rudyard Kipling spent their formative years locally, and Arthur Conan Doyle established a medical practice in the town in 1882. He wrote his first Sherlock Holmes story 'A Study in Scarlet' here in 1886, and eventually left Southsea in 1890.

◆

SOUTHSEA
Victoria Barracks 1898
Part of a large complex of military buildings, Victoria Barracks were built in 1880 and occupied by the King's Own Scottish Borderers until 1939. The barracks were taken over by the Royal Navy and finally demolished in the 1960s. The distinctive central tower was hit during the Second World War.

SOUTHSEA, VICTORIA BARRACKS 1898 42698

SOUTHSEA, ANCHOR OF HMS 'VICTORY' c1955 S161042

'England expects every man to do his duty'- Nelson's immortal words adorn the side of this stone plinth upon which stands the original anchor of HMS 'Victory'. Several notable monuments can also be seen on Clarence Esplanade, including the striking Naval War Memorial.

SOUTHSEA, CANOE LAKE c1955 S161049

One of Southsea's most famous landmarks is South Parade Pier, opened in 1879 and rebuilt in 1908 following a fire. Near it is the town's popular canoe lake, once part of the 'Great Morass', a pond on the heath that was once popular with snipe shooters.

SOUTHSEA, HOVERCRAFT C1965 S161123

SOUTHSEA
Hovercraft c1965
About six years before this photograph was taken, designer Christopher Cockerell was turning a drawing board dream into reality with his invention of the hovercraft, a revolutionary new concept in passenger travel. The Suffolk boat builder took out 56 patents on the design and the first experimental hovercraft crossed the English Channel in 1959.

◆

EMSWORTH
The Old Mill c1955
The old tide mill overlooking the quay at Emsworth, once Chichester Harbour's main port and an important centre for the oyster trade. Caroline, Princess of Wales, bathed in the sea here while staying at Emsworth in 1805, and the town had thoughts of becoming a royal watering place.

EMSWORTH, THE OLD MILL C1955 E62031

BURITON, THE VILLAGE 1898 41374
Edward Gibbon, the historian who wrote 'The Decline and Fall of the Roman Empire',
lived at the Manor House as a child. According to some sources, it was a visit to the ruins of ancient Rome that
inspired him to produce one of the great classics of English literature.

BURITON, THE POND 1898 41372
Located at the western extremity of the South Downs, Buriton captures the essence of the traditional English village. Overlooking the pond, at the eastern end of Buriton, is the village's tree-shaded Norman church, built of ironstone.

BUTSER HILL 1898 41367
Over the years sheep have grazed the slopes of this
famous chalk hill, which rises to 888 ft. The stamp of
ancient man is here too - there are traces of defensive
works on the summit, while on the lower flank are
Iron Age field boundaries or lynchets.

PETERSFIELD, FROM TILMORE 1906 54393

Petersfield is famous throughout Hampshire for several unusual street names. The Spain may have been named after Spanish wool merchants who gathered here to trade for wool and cloth, and Music Hill is where 18th-century military bands played.

PETERSFIELD, MARKET PLACE C1950 P48009

The most striking buildings in Petersfield are Georgian; some of them overlook the large square in which stands the statue of William III, depicted on horseback and dressed, absurdly, as a Roman. The statue, erected in 1753, was restored early in the 20th century. On the right is the Southdown Omnibus office.

STEEP
The Kettle Brook 1898

A short walk from The Harrow pub at Steep brings you to this delightful spot at the heart of hilly East Hampshire, sometimes described as 'Little Switzerland'. To the west lies the village centre and the partly Norman church of All Saints. The First World War poet Edward Thomas lived at nearby Berryfield Cottage.

◆

BRAMSHOTT
Tin Town 1917

Around the time this photograph was taken, the first of a series of Army camps was erected at Bramshott. The church-yard contains the graves of 330 Canadian soldiers; many of them died from an influenza epidemic which swept the area in 1917-18. On the right of the picture is the Church of England Soldiers Institute.

STEEP, KETTLESBROOK 1898 41362

BRAMSHOTT, TIN TOWN 1917 67987

BRAMSHOTT, QUINCE FARM 1917 67898
It was rural, bucolic scenes like this one at 600-acre Quince Farm that inspired Tennyson to write a poem of 47 words while visiting the area one summer's day in the 1860s. The parish of Bramshott includes some unusual place names, such as Hammer Bottom and Waggoners Wells.

LIPHOOK, THE ROYAL ANCHOR HOTEL 1924 75394

Standing in the shadow of a great chestnut tree, the Royal Anchor Hotel, once a posting and coaching house, dates from the time of Samuel Pepys who found 'good, honest people' here. Lord Nelson had breakfast here, and a young Queen Victoria and her mother, the Duchess of Kent, stayed overnight.

LIPHOOK, THE VILLAGE 1911 63110

Liphook expanded as a village thanks to the London-Portsmouth road and the arrival of the railway in 1859. The journey from the capital to the naval port by coach took eight hours; the six hours to Liphook cost 13s 6d.

LIPHOOK, NEW TOWN 1911 63116

Liphook had begun to expand by the time this photograph was taken; its streets were characterised by neat rows of Victorian and Edwardian houses. The sign on the step shows a monkey grabbing a bottle of lemonade. Further down is Plums Cycle Depot.

GRAYSHOTT, HEADLEY ROAD 1906 55572

A horse-drawn omnibus can be seen in the distance in this Edwardian photograph. Nine years before it was taken, a young Flora Thompson, who wrote the trilogy 'Lark Rise to Candleford', came to Grayshott to work at the post office. One of its customers was George Bernard Shaw, who rented a house in the village.

BORDON, THE VILLAGE 1919 68813
The distinctive onion dome above the premises of Frisby's Military Boot Stores is still a recognisable feature in Bordon today. Glass had to be specially made to fit the round window just below the dome.

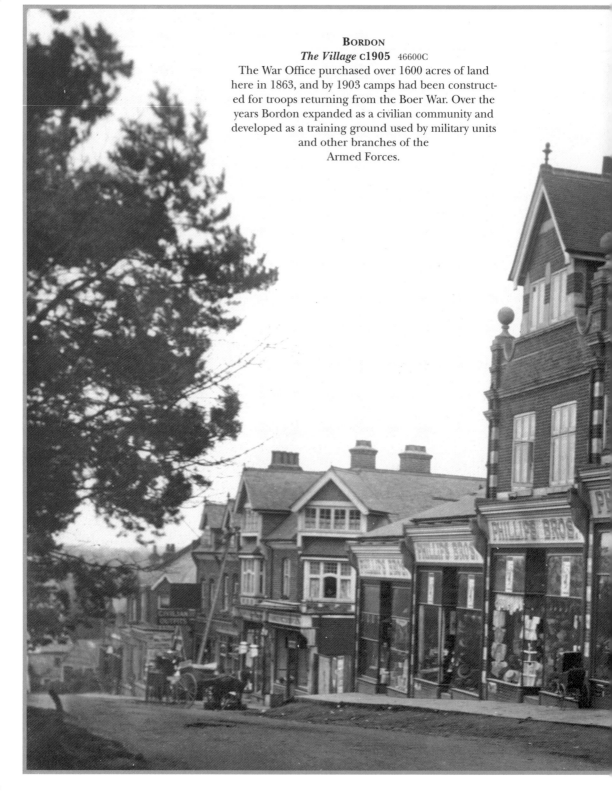

BORDON
The Village c1905 46600C
The War Office purchased over 1600 acres of land
here in 1863, and by 1903 camps had been constructed for troops returning from the Boer War. Over the
years Bordon expanded as a civilian community and
developed as a training ground used by military units
and other branches of the
Armed Forces.

CHAWTON, THE VILLAGE 1897 40739
Originally an inn, the house on the left of the picture is where Jane Austen lived during the last years of her life. The house, which was then called Chawton Cottage, was bought by her brother Edward.

CHAWTON, JANE AUSTEN'S HOUSE c1960 C530003
It was here that Jane Austen wrote 'Mansfield Park', 'Emma' and 'Persuasion'. The house, now a museum, has changed little over the years and includes her writing table, as well as a collection of documents and letters.

ALTON, MARKET STREET 1928 80818

At the close of the 19th century, Alton bore the stamp of an old country market town, with its bustling streets and striking shop fronts. Opposite the King's Head is the town's market square.

ALTON, HIGH STREET 1898 42266

Note the shopkeepers diligently scanning the High Street in search of custom. Outside E.W. Wrenn is a placard advertising the London Daily Chronicle; while Eiffel Tower lemonade is for sale at nearby Caffall & Co. This part of Alton includes various 18th-century buildings as well as some from an earlier period.

ALTON, NORMANDY STREET 1907 57239

Forty years before this picture was taken, a gruesome murder took place in Alton - that of Fanny Adams, an eight-year-old child. Her name later passed into the English language as 'Sweet Fanny Adams' or simply 'Sweet F.A'. Earlier still, the Roundheads captured the town from the Cavaliers during the Civil War.

ODIHAM, THE CHALK PIT 1903 49208

French soldiers were held as prisoners at Odiham during the Napoleonic wars, living in a camp dug out of an old chalk pit on the Alton road. According to some sources, they also helped to construct the nearby Basingstoke Canal. Odiham churchyard contains the graves of several French prisoners.

ODIHAM
The Canal Wharf **1906**
Completed in 1794, the Basingstoke Canal was originally planned to link London and Guildford with Southampton. Vessels plied the waterway carrying grain, coal, malt and farm produce. However, the canal's fortunes were never particularly good and eventually the western end was filled in. It later reopened following major restoration work.

◆

ODIHAM
Cemetery Hill **1910**
Odiham's houses are a mixture of Georgian and Tudor; some are timber-framed, which was common before local bricks came into general use in the 18th century. The Priory and neighbouring Palace Gate Farm were once part of a Tudor Palace visited by Queen Elizabeth I.

ODIHAM, THE CANAL WHARF 1906   55854

ODIHAM, CEMETERY HILL 1910   63011

YATELEY, THE COMMON 1924   75556

YATELEY
The Common 1924

Yateley Common, one of the largest commons in Hampshire, has long been famous in the area for Wyndham's Pool, an 18th-century fishpond reservoir. The Dartford Warbler is known to breed here, and the pool is also a favourite haunt of dragonflies. Smuggling was once a regular activity in the area.

COVE
The Village 1909

A typical Edwardian scene, with smartly dressed children looking coyly at the camera. A mile to the west lies Fleet Pond, Hampshire's largest freshwater lake. Between 1854 and 1972 it was used by the Army; prior to that it was a fishpond for the dean and chapter of Winchester Cathedral.

COVE, THE VILLAGE 1909   62079

BLACKWATER, THE VILLAGE 1906 57003
Blackwater, which shares its name with that of the river, lies just to the south of the Royal Military College at Sandhurst. On the right is the Red Lion and next to it are the premises of a baker and confectioner. Note the water trough for horses.

FARNBOROUGH, LYNCHFORD ROAD 1903 49319
The town of Farnborough has grown enormously over the years, mainly because of its close proximity to Aldershot. In this turn-of-the-century photograph soldiers can be seen marching into the distance while the Temperance Hotel offers suppers and beds and includes the Soldiers Cafe.

FARNBOROUGH
Lynchford Road **1919** 68913
This photograph depicts local residents out shopping in Farnborough. Many of the townsfolk would have been in the audience at Aldershot's famous Rushmoor Arena when military tattoos were staged there. The annual displays were first held in 1894, and were sometimes attended by as many as half a million people.

FARNBOROUGH, RECTORY LANE 1909 62076
This fascinating photograph shows an assortment of individuals all of whom appear to be mesmerised by the camera. There are bemused children, a caped policemen patrolling the area on horseback and a man sitting on a fence smoking a pipe. On the left of the picture there are signs of hedge cutting.

FARNBOROUGH, THE SCALA 1925 78118A
The wonderfully-titled 'Bardelys the Magnificent' was showing at The Scala when this photograph was taken. The ornately designed building is a vivid reminder of the days, long before the television and video age, when every town in the country had a picture house, or 'flea pit' as they were sometimes known.

ALDERSHOT, VICTORIA ROAD 1927 79623
On the right is the imposing facade of the old National Provincial Bank. The town of Aldershot is largely Victorian; in those early days some of the streets had shops on one side and barracks on the other. The older part of the town lies close to the railway station.

ALDERSHOT, UNION STREET 1918 68360
Four years after this photograph was taken, Aldershot became a borough. Union Street is littered with shop names and advertisements. On the left are signs for Frisby's Boot Stores - 'Best for Shoes, Best for All'. The adjacent dentist guarantees 'Absolutely Painless Extractions'.

Aldershot, Union Street 1935 86777

Burtons and Timothy Whites face one another across Union Street, drawing many shoppers to the town. However, Aldershot offers much more than shops. There is an extensive choice of military museums, including two in neighbouring Surrey.

Aldershot, Wellington Street 1892 31112

Before assuming the role of the first military town in Britain, Aldershot was no more than a pretty village comprising a church, a manor house and several farms, close to an area of open heathland.

ALDERSHOT
The Wellington Monument **1891**
One of the town's most famous landmarks is Matthew Wyatt's magnificent statue of Wellington on horseback. The Iron Duke, depicted here in bronze, originally stood at Hyde Park Corner in London before being dismantled piece by piece and transported to Aldershot by horses.

ALDERSHOT
Cambridge Military Hospital **1891**
Named after the Duke of Cambridge, Queen Victoria's uncle, this most distinguished of buildings opened as a military hospital in 1879 and remained in use for 117 years. Originally, each regiment had its own ward, with access from a corridor which extended for a quarter of a mile.

ALDERSHOT, THE WELLINGTON MONUMENT 1891   28673

ALDERSHOT, CAMBRIDGE MILITARY HOSPITAL 1891   28672

ALDERSHOT, THE SOLDIERS' HOME 1897 39504

The Soldiers' Home was established in 1863 and closed in 1961. Its purpose was to provide a recreational outlet for serving soldiers - somewhere other than a pub, where they could read, relax, have coffee and enjoy a period of quiet reflection. Its founder, Louisa Daniell, is buried in Aldershot military cemetery.

ALDERSHOT, THE INFANTRY BARRACKS 1891 28675

The glass canopy between the barracks enabled the soldiers to drill in the dry. However, the glass was difficult to keep clean and it was not uncommon for some squaddies to climb on the roof after a night's drinking. The barracks were demolished in 1961.

ALDERSHOT, THE SWIMMING POOL 1931 83887
As well as public parks and memorial gardens, Aldershot is famous for its enormous open-air swimming pool, which covers an acre and can hold a million gallons of water. These young ladies are looking coyly at the camera as they use the footsprays.

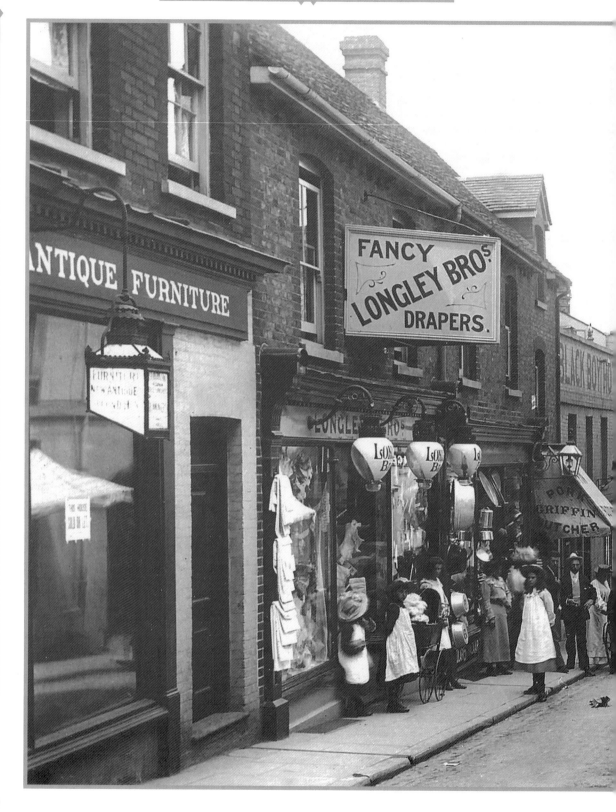

BASINGSTOKE
Church Street **1904** 52129
Church Street is busy with shoppers and shopkeepers.
Peeping above the town's rooftops is the tower of St
Michael the Archangel, perhaps the finest of
Hampshire's Perpendicular parish churches. Note the
sign on the right of the street in the shape of
a dustpan.

BASINGSTOKE, MARKET SQUARE C1955 B31008
Basingstoke's role as an important market centre dates back to medieval times; it was established as a borough in 1622 when James I granted the town a charter giving it a weekly market and a twice-yearly fair. By the late 17th century it was a prosperous market town.

BASINGSTOKE, LONDON STREET 1910 31329

Despite its somewhat drab image, Basingstoke has some interesting and distinctive buildings - particularly in Winchester Street and London Street. On the right is a striking 19th-century congregational church with a large Tuscan portico, while nearby are some almshouses founded in 1607 by Sir James Deane.

BASINGSTOKE, WINCHESTER STREET c1955 B31013

Note the old RAC logo on the front of the Wheatsheaf Hotel. The Wheatsheaf is still trading today, though no longer as a hotel. Next door are the premises of a pastry cook and confectioner.

BASINGSTOKE, HACKWOOD ROAD 1904 52127

As a town, Basingstoke has been growing since the early part of the 20th century, but in the last 40 years or so it has become the fastest growing town in Western Europe, its population increasing from 17,000 in the early 1950s to 67,000 in 1981.

BASINGSTOKE, OLD BASING VILLAGE 1898 42073

The village has long been famous for Basing House, a ruined building reduced to rubble by Cromwell and his army during the Civil War. St Mary's church, seen here, was also severely damaged, though extensive restoration work was undertaken in 1874. The church bells were removed by Cromwell.

BRAMLEY, THE MANOR HOUSE c1960 B696001

BRAMLEY
The Manor House c1960
The 16th-century half-timbered Manor House in Vyne Road fronts directly onto the road, so that its striking architecture, including carved bargeboards on the gables, can be studied at close quarters. Adjacent is a small Esso garage discreetly set back from the road.

◆

BRAMLEY
The Vyne c1960
One of Hampshire's finest houses, The Vyne was built between 1518 and 1527 by William Sandys who became Lord Chamberlain in 1526. John Leland, the 16th century antiquarian and scholar, described The Vyne as 'one of the principal houses in goodly building in all Hamptonshire'. The National Trust acquired the house in 1956.

BRAMLEY, THE VYNE c1960 B696032

Index

Frith Book Co Titles

www.francisfrith.co.uk

The Frith Book Company publishes over 100 new titles each year. A selection of those currently available is listed below. For latest catalogue please contact Frith Book Co.

Town Books 96 pages, approximately 100 photos. **County and Themed Books** 128 pages, approximately 150 photos (unless specified). All titles hardback with laminated case and jacket, except those indicated pb (paperback)

Title	ISBN	Price	Title	ISBN	Price
Amersham, Chesham & Rickmansworth (pb)	1-85937-340-2	£9.99	Devon (pb)	1-85937-297-x	£9.99
Andover (pb)	1-85937-292-9	£9.99	Devon Churches (pb)	1-85937-250-3	£9.99
Aylesbury (pb)	1-85937-227-9	£9.99	Dorchester (pb)	1-85937-307-0	£9.99
Barnstaple (pb)	1-85937-300-3	£9.99	Dorset (pb)	1-85937-269-4	£9.99
Basildon Living Memories (pb)	1-85937-515-4	£9.99	Dorset Coast (pb)	1-85937-299-6	£9.99
Bath (pb)	1-85937-419-0	£9.99	Dorset Living Memories (pb)	1-85937-584-7	£9.99
Bedford (pb)	1-85937-205-8	£9.99	Down the Severn (pb)	1-85937-560-x	£9.99
Bedfordshire Living Memories	1-85937-513-8	£14.99	Down The Thames (pb)	1-85937-278-3	£9.99
Belfast (pb)	1-85937-303-8	£9.99	Down the Trent	1-85937-311-9	£14.99
Berkshire (pb)	1-85937-191-4	£9.99	East Anglia (pb)	1-85937-265-1	£9.99
Berkshire Churches	1-85937-170-1	£17.99	East Grinstead (pb)	1-85937-138-8	£9.99
Berkshire Living Memories	1-85937-332-1	£14.99	East London	1-85937-080-2	£14.99
Black Country	1-85937-497-2	£12.99	East Sussex (pb)	1-85937-606-1	£9.99
Blackpool (pb)	1-85937-393-3	£9.99	Eastbourne (pb)	1-85937-399-2	£9.99
Bognor Regis (pb)	1-85937-431-x	£9.99	Edinburgh (pb)	1-85937-193-0	£8.99
Bournemouth (pb)	1-85937-545-6	£9.99	England In The 1880s	1-85937-331-3	£17.99
Bradford (pb)	1-85937-204-x	£9.99	Essex - Second Selection	1-85937-456-5	£14.99
Bridgend (pb)	1-85937-386-0	£7.99	Essex (pb)	1-85937-270-8	£9.99
Bridgwater (pb)	1-85937-305-4	£9.99	Essex Coast	1-85937-342-9	£14.99
Bridport (pb)	1-85937-327-5	£9.99	Essex Living Memories	1-85937-490-5	£14.99
Brighton (pb)	1-85937-192-2	£8.99	Exeter	1-85937-539-1	£9.99
Bristol (pb)	1-85937-264-3	£9.99	Exmoor (pb)	1-85937-608-8	£9.99
British Life A Century Ago (pb)	1-85937-213-9	£9.99	Falmouth (pb)	1-85937-594-4	£9.99
Buckinghamshire (pb)	1-85937-200-7	£9.99	Folkestone (pb)	1-85937-124-8	£9.99
Camberley (pb)	1-85937-222-8	£9.99	Frome (pb)	1-85937-317-8	£9.99
Cambridge (pb)	1-85937-422-0	£9.99	Glamorgan	1-85937-488-3	£14.99
Cambridgeshire (pb)	1-85937-420-4	£9.99	Glasgow (pb)	1-85937-190-6	£9.99
Cambridgeshire Villages	1-85937-523-5	£14.99	Glastonbury (pb)	1-85937-338-0	£7.99
Canals And Waterways (pb)	1-85937-291-0	£9.99	Gloucester (pb)	1-85937-232-5	£9.99
Canterbury Cathedral (pb)	1-85937-179-5	£9.99	Gloucestershire (pb)	1-85937-561-8	£9.99
Cardiff (pb)	1-85937-093-4	£9.99	Great Yarmouth (pb)	1-85937-426-3	£9.99
Carmarthenshire (pb)	1-85937-604-5	£9.99	Greater Manchester (pb)	1-85937-266-x	£9.99
Chelmsford (pb)	1-85937-310-0	£9.99	Guildford (pb)	1-85937-410-7	£9.99
Cheltenham (pb)	1-85937-095-0	£9.99	Hampshire (pb)	1-85937-279-1	£9.99
Cheshire (pb)	1-85937-271-6	£9.99	Harrogate (pb)	1-85937-423-9	£9.99
Chester (pb)	1-85937-382 8	£9.99	Hastings and Bexhill (pb)	1-85937-131-0	£9.99
Chesterfield (pb)	1-85937-378-x	£9.99	Heart of Lancashire (pb)	1-85937-197-3	£9.99
Chichester (pb)	1-85937-228-7	£9.99	Helston (pb)	1-85937-214-7	£9.99
Churches of East Cornwall (pb)	1-85937-249-x	£9.99	Hereford (pb)	1-85937-175-2	£9.99
Churches of Hampshire (pb)	1-85937-207-4	£9.99	Herefordshire (pb)	1-85937-567-7	£9.99
Cinque Ports & Two Ancient Towns	1-85937-492-1	£14.99	Herefordshire Living Memories	1-85937-514-6	£14.99
Colchester (pb)	1-85937-188-4	£8.99	Hertfordshire (pb)	1-85937-247-3	£9.99
Cornwall (pb)	1-85937-229-5	£9.99	Horsham (pb)	1-85937-432-8	£9.99
Cornwall Living Memories	1-85937-248-1	£14.99	Humberside (pb)	1-85937-605-3	£9.99
Cotswolds (pb)	1-85937-230-9	£9.99	Hythe, Romney Marsh, Ashford (pb)	1-85937-256-2	£9.99
Cotswolds Living Memories	1-85937-255-4	£14.99	Ipswich (pb)	1-85937-424-7	£9.99
County Durham (pb)	1-85937-398-4	£9.99	Isle of Man (pb)	1-85937-268-6	£9.99
Croydon Living Memories (pb)	1-85937-162-0	£9.99	Isle of Wight (pb)	1-85937-429-8	£9.99
Cumbria (pb)	1-85937-621-5	£9.99	Isle of Wight Living Memories	1-85937-304-6	£14.99
Derby (pb)	1-85937-367-4	£9.99	Kent (pb)	1-85937-189-2	£9.99
Derbyshire (pb)	1-85937-196-5	£9.99	Kent Living Memories(pb)	1-85937-401-8	£9.99
Derbyshire Living Memories	1-85937-330-5	£14.99	Kings Lynn (pb)	1-85937-334-8	£9.99

Available from your local bookshop or from the publisher

Frith Book Co Titles (continued)

Title	ISBN	Price	Title	ISBN	Price
Lake District (pb)	1-85937-275-9	£9.99	Sherborne (pb)	1-85937-301-1	£9.99
Lancashire Living Memories	1-85937-335-6	£14.99	Shrewsbury (pb)	1-85937-325-9	£9.99
Lancaster, Morecambe, Heysham (pb)	1-85937-233-3	£9.99	Shropshire (pb)	1-85937-326-7	£9.99
Leeds (pb)	1-85937-202-3	£9.99	Shropshire Living Memories	1-85937-643-6	£14.99
Leicester (pb)	1-85937-381-x	£9.99	Somerset	1-85937-153-1	£14.99
Leicestershire & Rutland Living Memories	1-85937-500-6	£12.99	South Devon Coast	1-85937-107-8	£14.99
Leicestershire (pb)	1-85937-185-x	£9.99	South Devon Living Memories (pb)	1-85937-609-6	£9.99
Lighthouses	1-85937-257-0	£9.99	South East London (pb)	1-85937-263-5	£9.99
Lincoln (pb)	1-85937-380-1	£9.99	South Somerset	1-85937-318-6	£14.99
Lincolnshire (pb)	1-85937-433-6	£9.99	South Wales	1-85937-519-7	£14.99
Liverpool and Merseyside (pb)	1-85937-234-1	£9.99	Southampton (pb)	1-85937-427-1	£9.99
London (pb)	1-85937-183-3	£9.99	Southend (pb)	1-85937-313-5	£9.99
London Living Memories	1-85937-454-9	£14.99	Southport (pb)	1-85937-425-5	£9.99
Ludlow (pb)	1-85937-176-0	£9.99	St Albans (pb)	1-85937-341-0	£9.99
Luton (pb)	1-85937-235-x	£9.99	St Ives (pb)	1-85937-415-8	£9.99
Maidenhead (pb)	1-85937-339-9	£9.99	Stafford Living Memories (pb)	1-85937-503-0	£9.99
Maidstone (pb)	1-85937-391-7	£9.99	Staffordshire (pb)	1-85937-308-9	£9.99
Manchester (pb)	1-85937-198-1	£9.99	Stourbridge (pb)	1-85937-530-8	£9.99
Marlborough (pb)	1-85937-336-4	£9.99	Stratford upon Avon (pb)	1-85937-388-7	£9.99
Middlesex	1-85937-158-2	£14.99	Suffolk (pb)	1-85937-221-x	£9.99
Monmouthshire	1-85937-532-4	£14.99	Suffolk Coast (pb)	1-85937-610-x	£9.99
New Forest (pb)	1-85937-390-9	£9.99	Surrey (pb)	1-85937-240-6	£9.99
Newark (pb)	1-85937-366-6	£9.99	Surrey Living Memories	1-85937-328-3	£14.99
Newport, Wales (pb)	1-85937-258-9	£9.99	Sussex (pb)	1-85937-184-1	£9.99
Newquay (pb)	1-85937-421-2	£9.99	Sutton (pb)	1-85937-337-2	£9.99
Norfolk (pb)	1-85937-195-7	£9.99	Swansea (pb)	1-85937-167-1	£9.99
Norfolk Broads	1-85937-486-7	£14.99	Taunton (pb)	1-85937-314-3	£9.99
Norfolk Living Memories (pb)	1-85937-402-6	£9.99	Tees Valley & Cleveland (pb)	1-85937-623-1	£9.99
North Buckinghamshire	1-85937-626-6	£14.99	Teignmouth (pb)	1-85937-370-4	£7.99
North Devon Living Memories	1-85937-261-9	£14.99	Thanet (pb)	1-85937-116-7	£9.99
North Hertfordshire	1-85937-547-2	£14.99	Tiverton (pb)	1-85937-178-7	£9.99
North London (pb)	1-85937-403-4	£9.99	Torbay (pb)	1-85937-597-9	£9.99
North Somerset	1-85937-302-x	£14.99	Truro (pb)	1-85937-598-7	£9.99
North Wales (pb)	1-85937-298-8	£9.99	Victorian & Edwardian Dorset	1-85937-254-6	£14.99
North Yorkshire (pb)	1-85937-236-8	£9.99	Victorian & Edwardian Kent (pb)	1-85937-624-X	£9.99
Northamptonshire Living Memories	1-85937-529-4	£14.99	Victorian & Edwardian Maritime Album (pb)	1-85937-622-3	£9.99
Northamptonshire	1-85937-150-7	£14.99	Victorian and Edwardian Sussex (pb)	1-85937-625-8	£9.99
Northumberland Tyne & Wear (pb)	1-85937-281-3	£9.99	Villages of Devon (pb)	1-85937-293-7	£9.99
Northumberland	1-85937-522-7	£14.99	Villages of Kent (pb)	1-85937-294-5	£9.99
Norwich (pb)	1-85937-194-9	£8.99	Villages of Sussex (pb)	1-85937-295-3	£9.99
Nottingham (pb)	1-85937-324-0	£9.99	Warrington (pb)	1-85937-507-3	£9.99
Nottinghamshire (pb)	1-85937-187-6	£9.99	Warwick (pb)	1-85937-518-9	£9.99
Oxford (pb)	1-85937-411-5	£9.99	Warwickshire (pb)	1-85937-203-1	£9.99
Oxfordshire (pb)	1-85937-430-1	£9.99	Welsh Castles (pb)	1-85937-322-4	£9.99
Oxfordshire Living Memories	1-85937-525-1	£14.99	West Midlands (pb)	1-85937-289-9	£9.99
Paignton (pb)	1-85937-374-7	£7.99	West Sussex (pb)	1-85937-607-x	£9.99
Peak District (pb)	1-85937-280-5	£9.99	West Yorkshire (pb)	1-85937-201-5	£9.99
Pembrokeshire	1-85937-262-7	£14.99	Weston Super Mare (pb)	1-85937-306-2	£9.99
Penzance (pb)	1-85937-595-2	£9.99	Weymouth (pb)	1-85937-209-0	£9.99
Peterborough (pb)	1-85937-219-8	£9.99	Wiltshire (pb)	1-85937-277-5	£9.99
Picturesque Harbours	1-85937-208-2	£14.99	Wiltshire Churches (pb)	1-85937-171-x	£9.99
Piers	1-85937-237-6	£17.99	Wiltshire Living Memories (pb)	1-85937-396-8	£9.99
Plymouth (pb)	1-85937-389-5	£9.99	Winchester (pb)	1-85937-428-x	£9.99
Poole & Sandbanks (pb)	1-85937-251-1	£9.99	Windsor (pb)	1-85937-333-x	£9.99
Preston (pb)	1-85937-212-0	£9.99	Wokingham & Bracknell (pb)	1-85937-329-1	£9.99
Reading (pb)	1-85937-238-4	£9.99	Woodbridge (pb)	1-85937-498-0	£9.99
Redhill to Reigate (pb)	1-85937-596-0	£9.99	Worcester (pb)	1-85937-165-5	£9.99
Ringwood (pb)	1-85937-384-4	£7.99	Worcestershire Living Memories	1-85937-489-1	£14.99
Romford (pb)	1-85937-319-4	£9.99	Worcestershire	1-85937-152-3	£14.99
Royal Tunbridge Wells (pb)	1-85937-504-9	£9.99	York (pb)	1-85937-199-x	£9.99
Salisbury (pb)	1-85937-239-2	£9.99	Yorkshire (pb)	1-85937-186-8	£9.99
Scarborough (pb)	1-85937-379-8	£9.99	Yorkshire Coastal Memories	1-85937-506-5	£14.99
Sevenoaks and Tonbridge (pb)	1-85937-392-5	£9.99	Yorkshire Dales	1-85937-502-2	£14.99
Sheffield & South Yorks (pb)	1-85937-267-8	£9.99	Yorkshire Living Memories (pb)	1-85937-397-6	£9.99

See Frith books on the internet at www.francisfrith.co.uk

FRITH PRODUCTS & SERVICES

Francis Frith would doubtless be pleased to know that the pioneering publishing venture he started in 1860 still continues today. Over a hundred and forty years later, The Francis Frith Collection continues in the same innovative tradition and is now one of the foremost publishers of vintage photographs in the world. Some of the current activities include:

Interior Decoration

Today Frith's photographs can be seen framed and as giant wall murals in thousands of pubs, restaurants, hotels, banks, retail stores and other public buildings throughout the country. In every case they enhance the unique local atmosphere of the places they depict and provide reminders of gentler days in an increasingly busy and frenetic world.

Product Promotions

Frith products are used by many major companies to promote the sales of their own products or to reinforce their own history and heritage. Frith promotions have been used by Hovis bread, Courage beers, Scots Porage Oats, Colman's mustard, Cadbury's foods, Mellow Birds coffee, Dunhill pipe tobacco, Guinness, and Bulmer's Cider.

Genealogy and Family History

As the interest in family history and roots grows world-wide, more and more people are turning to Frith's photographs of Great Britain for images of the towns, villages and streets where their ancestors lived; and, of course, photographs of the churches and chapels where their ancestors were christened, married and buried are an essential part of every genealogy tree and family album.

Frith Products

All Frith photographs are available Framed or just as Mounted Prints and Posters (size 23 x 16 inches). These may be ordered from the address below. From time to time other products - Address Books, Calendars, Table Mats, etc - are available.

The Internet

Already fifty thousand Frith photographs can be viewed and purchased on the internet through the Frith websites and a myriad of partner sites.

For more detailed information on Frith companies and products, look at these sites:

www.francisfrith.co.uk
www.francisfrith.com
(for North American visitors)

See the complete list of Frith Books at:

www.francisfrith.co.uk

This web site is regularly updated with the latest list of publications from the Frith Book Company. If you wish to buy books relating to another part of the country that your local bookshop does not stock, you may purchase on-line.

For further information, trade, or author enquiries please contact us at the address below:
The Francis Frith Collection, Frith's Barn, Teffont, Salisbury, Wiltshire, England SP3 5QP.
Tel: +44 (0)1722 716 376 Fax: +44 (0)1722 716 881 Email: sales@francisfrith.co.uk

See Frith books on the internet at www.francisfrith.co.uk

FREE MOUNTED PRINT

Mounted Print
Overall size 14 x 11 inches

Fill in and cut out this voucher and return
it with your remittance for £2.25 (to cover postage and handling). Offer valid for delivery to UK addresses only.

Choose any photograph included in this book.
Your SEPIA print will be A4 in size. It will be mounted in a cream mount with a burgundy rule line (overall size 14 x 11 inches).

**Order additional Mounted Prints
at HALF PRICE (only £7.49 each*)**
If you would like to order more Frith prints from this book, possibly as gifts for friends and family, you can buy them at half price (with no additional postage and handling costs).

Have your Mounted Prints framed
For an extra £14.95 per print* you can have your mounted print(s) framed in an elegant polished wood and gilt moulding, overall size 16 x 13 inches (no additional postage and handling required).

---

* IMPORTANT!

These special prices are only available if you order at the same time as you order your free mounted print. You must use the ORIGINAL VOUCHER on this page (no copies permitted). We can only despatch to one address.

Send completed Voucher form to:
The Francis Frith Collection, Frith's Barn, Teffont, Salisbury, Wiltshire SP3 5QP

CHOOSE ANY IMAGE FROM THIS BOOK

Please do not photocopy this voucher. Only the original is valid, so please fill it in, cut it out and return it to us with your order.

Picture ref no	Page no	Qty	Mounted @ £7.49	Framed + £14.95	Total Cost
		1	Free of charge*	£	£
			£7.49	£	£
			£7.49	£	£
			£7.49	£	£
			£7.49	£	£
			£7.49	£	£

Please allow 28 days for delivery	* Post & handling (UK)	£2.25
	Total Order Cost	£

Title of this book . . . .

I enclose a cheque/postal order for £ . . . .
made payable to 'The Francis Frith Collection'

OR please debit my Mastercard / Visa / Switch / Amex card
(credit cards please on all overseas orders), details below

Card Number

Issue No (Switch only)   Valid from (Amex/Switch)

Expires   Signature

Name Mr/Mrs/Ms . . . .

Address . . . .

. . . .

. . . .

. . . . Postcode . . . .

Daytime Tel No . . . .

Email . . . .

Valid to 31/12/05

Would you like to find out more about Francis Frith?

We have recently recruited some entertaining speakers who are happy to visit local groups, clubs and societies to give an illustrated talk documenting Frith's travels and photographs. If you are a member of such a group and are interested in hosting a presentation, we would love to hear from you.

Our speakers bring with them a small selection of our local town and county books, together with sample prints. They are happy to take orders. A small proportion of the order value is donated to the group who have hosted the presentation. The talks are therefore an excellent way of fundraising for small groups and societies.

Can you help us with information about any of the Frith photographs in this book?

We are gradually compiling an historical record for each of the photographs in the Frith archive. It is always fascinating to find out the names of the people shown in the pictures, as well as insights into the shops, buildings and other features depicted.

If you recognize anyone in the photographs in this book, or if you have information not already included in the author's caption, do let us know. We would love to hear from you, and will try to publish it in future books or articles.

Our production team

Frith books are produced by a small dedicated team at offices in the converted Grade II listed 18th-century barn at Teffont near Salisbury, illustrated above. Most have worked with the Frith Collection for many years. All have in common one quality: they have a passion for the Frith Collection. The team is constantly expanding, but currently includes:

Jason Buck, John Buck, Ruth Butler, Heather Crisp, David Davies, Isobel Hall, Julian Hight, Peter Horne, James Kinnear, Karen Kinnear, Tina Leary, Stuart Login, Amanda Lowe, David Marsh, Sue Molloy, Kate Rotondetto, Dean Scource, Eliza Sackett, Terence Sackett, Sandra Sampson, Adrian Sanders, Sandra Sanger, Julia Skinner, Claire Tarrier, Lewis Taylor, Shelley Tolcher and Lorraine Tuck.